BOA
EDITIONS LTD

THEOPHOBIA

THEOPHOBIA

Poems by
BRUCE BEASLEY

AMERICAN POETS CONTINUUM SERIES, No. 136

BOA EDITIONS, LTD. ✻ ROCHESTER, NY ✻ 2012

First Edition
12 13 14 15 7 6 5 4 3 2 1

For information about permission to reuse any material from this book please contact The Permissions Company at www.permissionscompany.com or e-mail permdude@eclipse. net.

Publications by BOA Editions, Ltd.—a not-for-profit corporation under section 501 (c) (3) of the United States Internal Revenue Code—are made possible with funds from a variety of sources, including public funds from the New York State Council on the Arts, a state agency; the Literature Program of the National Endowment for the Arts; the County of Monroe, NY; the Lannan Foundation for support of the Lannan Translations Selection Series; the Mary S. Mulligan Charitable Trust; the Rochester Area Community Foundation; the Arts & Cultural Council for Greater Rochester; the Steeple-Jack Fund; the Ames-Amzalak Memorial Trust in memory of Henry Ames, Semon Amzalak and Dan Amzalak; and contributions from many individuals nationwide. See Colophon on page 108 for special individual acknowledgments.

ART WORKS.
arts.gov

State of the Arts

NYSCA

Cover Design: Sandy Knight
Cover Art: Mark Rothko (1903–1970) © ARS, NY. Crucifix, 1941–42. Oil on canvas, 27 x 23 in.
Interior Design and Composition: Richard Foerster
BOA Logo: Mirko

Library of Congress Cataloging-in-Publication Data

Beasley, Bruce, 1958–
Theophobia : poems / by Bruce Beasley. — 1st ed.
    p. cm. — (American Poets Continuum Series ; 136)
"for Suzanne and Jin."
ISBN 978-1-934414-91-0 (pbk.)
I. Title.
PS3552.E1748T47 2012
811'.54—dc23
                                    2012014337

BOA Editions, Ltd.
250 North Goodman Street, Suite 306
Rochester, NY 14607
www.boaeditions.org
A. Poulin, Jr., Founder (1938–1996)

Contents

for Suzanne and Jin

my pearls of great price
perfect love casteth out fear —First Epistle of John, 4:18

One might ask why, if the universe is indeed a secret book of the gods with a coded message for us, this message is not written in ordinary language rather than in hieroglyphics whose decoding is discouragingly arduous and, above all, never results in certainty. But this question is futile, for two independent reasons. First, it assumes that we do know, or can imagine, what the universe would be like if its message and meaning were clearly readable and unambiguously displayed before our eyes. But we do not know this, and we lack the kind of imagination necessary to imagine it. Second, it is possible that if we knew why *the message is hidden, or partly hidden, it would no longer be hidden—in other words, that concealment of the reasons for which it is hidden is a necessary part of its being hidden.*

—Leszek Kołakowski, *Metaphysical Horror*

The dread of the Lord is the beginning of wisdom.

—Proverbs 1:7

ONE

(Pilgrim's Deviations 1)

The holy orders' indistinguishable
susurruses, then
the setting-forth, the in-

direction:
first toward crux,
then lux,
then x.

I'll say the Nones at 3, the Crucifixion hour.

No Dies Irae, no hours-of-spleen, no tenderness-minutes, no said graces.
No charred sins set out upon the water.

Kyrie
eleison, whatever
You find unburnt here.

Having Read the Holy Spirit's Wikipedia

1.

Glossolalic and disincarnate, interfere
in me, interleave me
and leave me through my breathing: like some third

person conjugation I've rewhispered
in a language I keep trying to learn, a tongue
made only of verbs, and all its verbs irregular.

2.

I've been Googling You lately, for some slipped-
loose theoinwardness You've come
to mean, some comfort of Third Person

held as breath, but I can't keep
straight sometimes which one of You
is You:

there's One who fractures off from light
as light, I know, and One
(is that One You?) *eternally begotten*, so never not at just that instant
        being born.

3.

Being-Without-a-Body, get
to me
and shiver along the nerves

like the *Toxoplasma gondii* parasite
that works its way deep up a rat's brain
and lays its cysts all through the amygdala,

unsnips the dendrites from networks
of instinctive fear that repel
the rat from cat pheromones, and reconnects

the wiring so the rat's testes swell
with attraction at the smell
of cat-piss and so urge the rat straight toward

the predator's mouth, since a cat-gut's
the only place where toxoplasma can breed, and the parasite leaves
the cat's body in the feces another rat will eat

and that rat's brain will also be restrung
from dread to lust for what consumes it: Spirit
of Holy Fear, who's afraid?

      4.

If You're in me I don't feel it.
Say Your verb, Your *let-there-be*
deep in *my* amygdala's fear-circuits, speak in me

through the X of Lexapro, its
self-cancellable crux:
tell me about light-from-light, serotonin-

from-synaptic-cleft, tell something about a long
half-life and Your charged
indwelling in the cells.

Here comes Pentecost, that
anti-Easter (one of You up-
vanished, and One come

down, in flame-
from-lingual-flame, that sacral
lick of redescent).

Say me Your babelwords then,
self-tripled One, under
the mind's reruined ziggurat.

5.

Because doves have no gall bladder
they have come
to stand for mildness. They stand

for You, warble, blue
underwing-flash and quaver, con-
and in-substantial

Squab of the Holy Ghost.
Some Ark's scraping some
mud-ridged, just-dried Ararat now

inside me, some dove's
dropped an olive sprig on its bow, meant to stand
once more for the passing of the gall.

6.

Blood-dad,
my son's friend asked me, *are you
his blood-dad?*

You're no blood-dad, not Yahweh's
hail-curse or locust-flock or Sodom-
smolder, nor Christ-

of-Blisters with His gall-cup
and Shroud-stare, Holy Foreskin
over whose ring of blood You dove-

coo and brood,
not the Father from whom You merely,
mystically, continuously, *proceed*—

I'm no blood-dad, either, I'm adoptive, *Joseph's
not Jesus' birth-dad*, my son told me
when I read him the Nativity

"for that which is conceived in her
is of the Holy Ghost":
so Jesus' dad was just like you . . .

7.

Through "spiration" and not "generation" You are said
to *proceed*, but the question of Who ex-pires You—
Father or Son, or both—has led to a thousand years of anathema and
    schism.

The Wikipedia on just that question goes twenty pages.
Ungenerative, ungenerated, You're like me: recessive and proceeding
    nonetheless, like the wick's
wax-wet and sizzle as it hardens into self-douse.

8.

Explorer has encountered
an unexpected error
and needs to close.

9.

Fricative, constrictive, like a gush
of burnt scrapwood smoke from a neighbor's yard,
its wintercleared thornbushes and rattlesticks in firepit,

greencrackle and sap-hiss, late March Lent-smoke,
ash-smack in back of tongue and eyes, forehead-and-cheek streak of
        char.
Numinous, pneumatic, Who

bloweth where You listeth, Whom
the world will never know, list to blow
down me.

Year's End Paradoxography

paradoxography: an ancient literary genre composed of lists of occurrences considered bizarre, abnormal, portentous, miraculous, and inexplicable.

> *How wonderful that we have met with a paradox. Now we have some hope of making progress.*
> —Niels Bohr

—If you'd like to talk to a live person, just say "live person,"

says the robot-voice on the TiVo Customer Service line.
—Live person, I say.
—Hmmnn . . . I'm not sure I got that.
—Would you like to talk with a live person, or continue working with me?

—No. Live person, please.
—Hmmnn . . . I'm still not sure I got that . . .

X

As a kid I always thought it went
*Our Father which aren't
in heaven,* and sat
staring at His stained-glass throne, wondering
where instead He were.

X

Because of the near
indistinguishability of *1* and *l,*

it kept saying: *Enter the alphanumeric
or hexadecimal code,*

it kept saying: *To continue you must reenter the code.*

X

Some assembly's required. The wireless network's
unsecured, its password
still unchanged from the default
password, its already-forgotten login either
Orthodox or *paradox.*

X

In passing it was mentioned that the dead
could be expected no longer to arise.

X

The witness said *subpoena* instead of *penis, penis*
instead of *vagina.*

X

Are there extralexical elements here, and if so, how are they to be
written?

X

The Very Reverend Metropolitan and Primate
has adjudicated the situation, and the liturgy's
ancient reiterations have been stilled.

An alarming lack of catechesis has been fingered.

The gold-enameled garb is hung in a chancellery,
and the incense's snuffer
smolders.

X

Wait, the gas cap warns
me, *until the hissing stops.*

X

As cervix to vagina, so the Law's
letter, to its spirit.

X

The siccative packet in a shoe box
read, unaccountably, *Do not eat.*

X

Although I have the confirmation code,
they said they could not use it to confirm
any of the particulars of my account.

X

He inserted his vagina into my subpoena.

X

*Are there any further
difficulties,*
the psychiatrist asked her,
listing while she sobbed.

X

Take, the medicine bottle advises,
*until distress
subsides.*

X

She said *oh* for *zero,* she said
my set for her breasts and *his package* for her lover's genitalia.

X

He'd never really understood the difference
between contractions and possessives
but knew to call a doctor if contractions
came ten minutes apart.

He'd always secretly wondered why if *is* was
the present tense they always called it
the *verb-to-be,* as if it hadn't yet arrived,
and if that was what led to all
its present
tension.

X

What is this word *decussate?* This cross, this deca-, this 10, this
chi, this intersect, this eliminator, this ancient, formidable X?

X

The sung liturgy's reiterant
in the mind: *We who mystically*
represent
re pre sent
the cherubim
re pre sent
the che e e ru bim
now lay aside all earthly cares . . .

O terra infirma. The confirmation
code will confirm—

on earth or heaven—
no transaction.

X

Take, until distress subsides.
Until the difficulties,
one by one, subside.

X

I'm not sure I got
that: did that sign
say *God is nowhere*
or *God is now here,*
or both?

X

Live person,
please.

Because some days *being* feels
experimental, randomized,
placebo-suspect, double-blind,

some voice inside the hissing
keeps saying to us (robotic, anachronistic): *Reenter the code.*

TWO

(Pilgrim's Deviations 2)

The cross's stations lie
everywhere, mundo-
intolerant.

Is it claustral where You issue from,

where You'd sequester me
diminished among the shriven, what
part of who they were remains?

Me and You
are like heterographs:
the difference, say,
between the sound of the g in God
and the one in naught.

All Saints

The demystification
unfurls. Arcana, manifestly
occult, are no more
at our disposal.
The xenotransplantation
of the vatic
into the vernacular
has been halted pending further
investigation. All's
serioburlesque & subcelestial.
& all these mantic
enigmas of the banal:
liturgy's polyglot
& thrice-holy hymn,
oracle bones charred in crematoria.
The side effects of placebo—
gastric spasms, bronchial
ache, cicada-whirr
far-down in the ear—fail,
over time, to ameliorate.
Some magus holds his chalice
under a spigot's burble & spurt.
The Venus flytrap seals
shut its three spiked mouths.

The Kingdom of God Is Not Usher'd In with Pomp and Exclamations

---

No man, when he hath lighted a candle, covereth it with a vessel, or putteth it under a bed; but setteth it on a candlestick, that they that enter in might see the light. For nothing is secret, that shall not be made manifest.

—Luke 8: 16–17

1.

Soweth the sower
word—

the swelled then
scarified then split
seed coat,

hillsides all furrowed and dunged:

and so troublous
matter arises.

2.

And the seerstones pass over the tablets.
Weren't you told yet to trance-
scribe your History as it comes?
Already bunched germ-shoots
just after the plough, these
volunteer creeplings:

3.

Much crop will conceal the land.
Rewet your quill, for the grain's
tassels go shrivel-white.

4.

Those who have have
taken from me, who Am
Not, who would not be.

5.

These parables, these
gleanings from recondite
similarities:
secrets
of the Kingdom, which
all the stories made
to tell them undermade.

6.

The history of emergency starts within.
Like the wind, which is no more
than the shivering in the grain
its passing exposes.

These candles: you must
set them under your bed,
so their shadow-rips, wax-
hisses, their six sputtering

balefires lavish your un-
lovemaking and then

your spasms of sleep.

Sunrise Insomnia Service

Gethsemane's sleepers, be with me
if I sleep.

Hypnopomps to the cock's crow,
to the olive grove's

dawnshadows' undergnarl.

Skull-Place, tricrossed, two-thieved hill,
over-

hang me if I wake.

†

The bed-world
is the total part,

unrememberable mnemonics
muttered through the dream

(Now I lay me,
tarry here awhile—

now I lay me
down—tarry here

with me awhile,
and wait, and watch)—

Sleep-horde, sleep's
grace-hoard, reinterred, salt-preserved.

†

Anti-
heliotropic
garden-sleeper:
somnotropic, thanatropic, oneirotrope—

It's too late now, the waker said, *sleep on, sleep on, the hour's already at hand.*

†

Wash, Lord, Your
hands of me.
            Take
the wine-sponge, myrrhed
and galled, vinegared,
at the sword's tip, when I
won't thirst.

Take the rood, if I refuse
to stagger as You please.

Unloose me,
unaccountably:

Barabbas me . . .

Stray Apostrophes

---

for the unwritten

i.

Supplicant, your petitions

bear no words: overheard
and underheard

celebrant of the dirge.

ii.

Namelord, syllables'
cosmos' ever-accelerant spew.

Many-laureled and ill-known.

iii.

Heaped
wasp-hive's chambers

blue-inflected

and swarmable just across the stained glass.

Untranslatable phrases—their
hard italic slant

(*eyheh asher ehyeh*), their meant

unmean.

Say *shibboleth,*
Supplicant, and pass,

liturgical and sibylline, go my way.

Meaning-seethe and -sieve

Unhearable

hurt melody, adjective
and adjective inclining toward no noun.

Your petitions
de-spell themselves.

Whose
Once upon a time (and times, and half a time)
I would hold myself

awake for till half-dawn . . .

viii.

Shriver
behind the grillwork,

penitent
or accuser, avoid
the *near occasions*

of thy sin.

Confiteor: absolution's
muffled mouth.

ix.

And what *termination shock*
in this solar wind

as it shoves back the interstellar

swath of cosmic rays—
shock of heliopause before the extrasolar

wandering

when

the orbiting of you is broken.

x.

Afterflowering: desiccated pod's

milk and blue-gray seed, its split-
opening, at last, its windward

pour—

xi.

Wreathe me with what: whatnot, what's.

Verb
in the flame, anonymous

and obliquitous be thy name.

Reading the Not-Written

agrapha (not written): the sayings of Jesus not in the Bible

i.

A papyrus leaf
from the desert trash-heap's

mutilated oracle,
with one word left there of some

outspired holy utterance: *Poverty,*
saith the moth-eaten Saying.

ii.

By what schema has the rhapsode stitched together the song

& the agrapha been stricken from the gospel & left wandering
from lips to unhallowed lips, out of papyrus-

rips, the no-longer-sanctified places
where worms ate through the scroll

just where Christ opened his mouth to speak
or wrote into the dirt

       You have received mercy [. . .] *become*
   they wrote [. . .] *book, as* [. . .] *to you again* [. . .] *and just as*
   they [. . .] *hear and* [. . .] *they* [. . .] *understand. Do you not*
desire, then, to be filled?

iii.

& so says the known-
to-be-corrupted text:
There is nothing buried which shall not be known.

iv.

Poverty

v.

Legei Iesous, Jesus say
the unwritten scripture, the lost
matter of the verso & recto, let it
come, heretical & legitimized at last.

vi.

Reader,
say to me the doubted Sayings
never heard, from the scattered codex,
the Sayings never found yet in the mummy-wraps of cats,
the hierophant Sayings in the still-unreadable glyph

of a dead language.
Rhapsode who never knew
that's what you were,
open the amulet in your mind & read me what talisman text
has hung there, legible
& unauthorized, all your life.

THREE

(Pilgrim's Deviations 3)

These ex-votos, these
scattered word-vows: take
and incinerate them,

as You will.

To have harmonized those eventide hymns
a cappella, as it's done in the chapel,
a defuncta, as they no longer choose to sing

here in the AllSurround
temple, the Nullum-
theon.

I want to go
where it is ago's gone,
to the escape-scape, the scrub and shrub of it,

I want to go
as what I am,
unadorer, an-
aphrodisiac, not-yet

inorganic.

Valedictions

little missives against your going

—The wheels retract and newly
de-iced, sleet-
hit wings
shiver now into the arc
of your casting-out,

thy going unenough

—Oh Nowhere-
Near, oh Xenos, who

knew we'd be divisible
so evenly, with no carried-over

remainder

—I am to you a currency
devalued, then defunct
then collectable among
cabinets of curiosity, some
access-forbidden archival vault

—Insomniac, what aubadal
song when you don't wake

having unslept

what shred
of snatching-you-
back-from-night

clung in my hand

—Have you continued to feel
filaments of chill

Are the utterative possibilities already exhausted
Do even questions leave

not anymore their mark

—What is this thing
between us, its
morph and drip and fang

its escape and stompings-yon, its
ill-understood
agon and undemise

—You are to me as what's made
in love is
to the humdrum means of its production

—If we could make ourselves some housed
and inhuddled figurines, prayer-
poised toward each other, some
shrine we haven't figured
out yet

how to erect

—Little uncancellable voice of 4 A.M.

A permanent intermission
will follow this closing act

There will be no further announcements. Listen, hard

—Away
from speech, *apo-*

logize, are we
now at apogee

that orbit point
most recoiled

from what draws in

"*Apo-* marks things

detached or separate"
so cast

away from me, abide
with me: let's each

apologize, all disattached
(as we must be now)

from speech

—Death-sentence me

like the lichen splotched on fir limbs
that spells out the wood's inner
irreversible process of decay

—Some Documents of Separation
unfileable, uncertifiable
their edges singed, their broken
contract language melted inward, word
ashcrumbling over charred word

—You were to me as trout-mouth
was to lure, to temporary air

You *are* to me   caesural

—These missives you won't read
missals

we don't pray
Let's write this

divisibility

off, as
if our losses

were only on paper

—Still the little wintersquall-
scuttled ferryboats between us

Do not forget to shutter the storm windows
Do not forget to gather
what children there
still are

in

Theme and Invariants

So you see I've begun looking after you

looking *for* you

looking for *you*, who would not see
as relentlessly as I did
what we both meant
to end

So that you see just as long as you're made
to listen
to this lyre's
sedulous strain

Whose head severed in the river-current,
unlooked-at & still singing
all its way downstream to Lesbos

Not stopped *looking* after
you'd already begun to look twice
in every direction but ours

So I turned back too, back to
what we'd both been looking
away from, looking
for

looking *after,* in this
aftermath of whatever
we end up calling
what we ended

So you see
I've begun
relooking
so that you see

(pluck and pluck of the lyre)

So you see I've begun
again
(silt
under the eyelids,
silt on the singing tongue)

looking after you

The Scale by Which the Mapped Concerns the Map

1.   We are the map's
icons, the clot-
black or gray hyphen-
lines, the capital's
isolate circled star.

The key
boxed underneath
in the smallest font will tell
us exactly what it is we mean

to stand for.

2.   Is there no difference
between a *legend*
and a *key.*

We've never known
a scale of more
than one to one,
imperceptible dis-
proportion . . .

3.   And here we are again, self-within:
legended,
aliased and atlased.

4.   Without its scale, the map's
a sumptuary object,
quarter-inch a thousand miles, a yard a sliver
of off-green.

I'd chart your inwardness but where's the key.
The scale-pan's weight subtractable from the measure.

5.   If the scale is an arrangement of our notes

and what's left inaudible between them

6.   As diagnosis
is to disease,

so the map's
legend, to the mapped.

7.   All we do, Libra, is practice
at our scales,

finger the frets
toward some unlearned nocturne's diminishment, its flats.

8.   Will the key
reexplain
everything on the mapface that's been

inscrutably abbreviated?

9.   Legend is to history as map is to its legend.

10.   We've grown

so tired of persistent direction—
is there still some way

to unmap
each other that
the scales

might fall from our eyes?

11.   Then say
to me something

I can't expect, or negotiate-
against, or boundary-draw:

draw me a map wherein

no legend's
legible, or needed.

FOUR

(Pilgrim's Deviations 4)

Oh Holy-of-Unholies I followed the detailed
inset map toward You
but never could find the juncture
from it to the vaguer, rumpled,
folded and refolded, surrounding small-scale map that leads

someplace real.

Genomic Vanitas

§

(Vanitas)

Of thy last end, in all thy works, be mindful
the still life's legend says:

lyre & death's-head clock, depetalling
tulip & convolvulus-canker,

wrought silver candle-snuffer,
& fruit flies' agitated sphere

over split skin of cherries & blue-mold
caved-in scab on folds of peach:

in each, unwound, ripped-in-half
strands of DNA

self-duplicate &, replicant, endure their going-hence:
double-helixed

surrogate of the everlasting, like Eternity
in the tail-whip of gamete, in the condom's

spermicidal tip.

§

(Vocation)

        —& all this millennium-turn a dispossession
of the mind, its

overmurmuring by the slurred
vernacular of half-

comprehended genome, unassimilable
underlanguage of synapse & chromosomal litter—

Its words—*pseudogene, selfish sequence, mutagenesis*—
half penetralia to me & half gloss:

As if the exegesis—of DNA's
scripture & scat—could ever cease.

As though some ineradicable trait
translated out of the incoherent

lingua prima of gene could tear

my *self* apart, mitotic, strand by strand—

Like the irritable
switching of a medley, melody
blended & disarranged, interrupted
into scramble & impatient merge:
the lability of these helices,
exon & intron, *code & junk.*

Can't we say
anymore, with Descartes, *the soul
can work independently of the brain,*
can we say anymore, with Descartes,

ignoramus et ignorabimus, we are ignorant
and shall so remain?

Tell me, snipped thread, warped ladder,
what it is you say I am.
Nucleus-cosmographer, hymn me
the six-billion-lettered song of self.

§

(Void Domiciles)
—Odyssey XI

Necromance
of you, father & mother: what spell
in each cell summons you back

in me—UUU for phenylalanine,
CAA for glutamine,
CGC for arginine

& a UGA for *Stop*—

   —Twenty-five years since, both of you
drunk to the death.
What tangle of crossed-over
chromosomes encodes still your long-
gone-to-humus lust into my skin?

(Skin cells
that will be shed for you
on everything I touch—)

Underworld-
ferriers, in amino acid chains
of proteins, a billion
codons in every nucleus

I take from you, in every
craving I take from you:

How came you here
to linger—as if surviving—
in the gloomy shade
of my every cell?

—& you answer, in tandem, in doubled
chromosomes:
—*My own unspeakable*
excess in wine

sealed me here, in the void domiciles of Dis . . .

§

(Mother Tongue)

Ninety-eight percent
of our DNA is junk,

uncipherable stutter
of the genome—

By the alias of gibberish it goes,
mother tongue's

stammer of non sequitur & unsense
nuclear-deep,

dittography's
irrelevant insistence & irrelevant

in*in*sistence, in-
*ininin*sistence . . .

—Cytonaut,

oracle-supplicant, read
us & read us again

this accident, these vocables at the core.

§

(Like Begets Unlike)

Incorruptible,

like begets like, till the mutant
& discontinuous
anti-unanimity in the coding

becomes heritable in the germ:

& *unlikelihood* & *unlikeness*
corrupt their way through the genome,
zygote's trillions of cells

bearing the newmade
& alien
gene into the world,

extravagation & singular defect . . .

§

(Nothing to Obstruct)

Shall there be
frogs & mice without brains? *Nihil obstat.* Circumcision
foreskin snippets to patch together a new face
for the burned? *Nihil obstat.*

Unfeathered chickens to save on cooling bills?
    Nihil obstat.
A cactus growing human hair? *Nihil obstat.*

Human embryos dangling as earrings?
            :Obstat. Contra naturam.

*Nature sometimes draws aside & goes
away, & in these remote parts indulges herself*

in shy & hidden excesses . . .

§

(Memento Vivi)

*The only structure linking
man to God,*
Dali said of DNA—

In-spiral in in-spiral, spoke & spoke—

Today I have been reading
the genome of the Plague:
GCG
ACG
ATC
ACC . . .

            —Nucleotide
on nucleotide, carbon
nitrogen phosphorus,
rat to flea to bloodborne
pathogen. To mind. *And in this flea
our two bloods mingled be,* buboes
surging in armpit & groin . . .

The plague full swift goes by;
I am sick, I must die—

So we divine
deviance, Dali,
in nature: evolvable augur.
Let there be

this sequencing
of genomes, *do this*
in memory

that in these cell-montages we still *live—*
shuffle of base pairs on the gene, bacterium to us, burnt-
out telomeres in ultraviolet light—
memento vivi, remember
already-dead
Dolly, timepiece
crawling down the wall.

§

(Canticle of the Creatures)
—after St. Francis

Of You most high, he bears

the likeness: fruit fly in the lab, praised be you
of the gene for eyes forced to expression
so they sprout, ectopic
& photosensitive,
on antennae & wing & all six legs, oh 14-eyed
& totipotent seer, gene
turned everywhere on . . .

All praise is yours, OncoMouse™
of tumorigenesis & induced mutation

who bears our flaws in your overfecund tissues,
with a human oncogene
guaranteed in each of your cells,
you *reliably develop neoplasms*
in the mammaries, and so bear
commercially our sister, bodily death.

Be praised, transgenic
pig of microinjected
human growth hormone genes,
with your *deleterious effects*
of deformed skull & pneumonia
(*& the unclean spirits went out*
& entered into the swine),
with your reduced carcass
fat & low cholesterol
tenderloin, by whom
He gives His creatures nourishment.

Be praised, Alba, phosphorescent
rabbit, jellyfish genes in your albescent hide,
and our brother mouse, with human ear
sprouting out of his side.

Altissimo,
Omnipotente, with great humility
we hold our nucleic
acids to theirs—cuttlefish,
slime mold, *E. coli*, bruiseless
tomato:

& to Yours, o likeness of our likeness, all
totipotent & blessed, mitochondrion
to mitochondrion, mutation
to mutation, codon

to gibberish, same, same, & (Argus-eyed, omniscopic) the same.

§

(Reading About Retrotransposons in Amish Country, in the Fall)

Cockcrow & cricket-scrape, dried
cornhusk at roadside, buggy-horse-gnawed
& rent down the middle like a helix in mid-mitosis—

It's said that certain genes can leap
from chromosome to chromosome, from
parasite to host (*for yea, ye shall be*

strangers, & also exiles) & so
accelerate the trans-
blending & the swap—

(grasshopper-shiver through prairie grass,
fiber optic cable buried
under a buggy barn)

So this is no point
mutation, no single shift in the code, but a full
shuffle halfway through the deal—

Thou art a stranger oh gypsy
gene, o wanderer, oh jumping
retrotransposon, from

virus to leafcutter to sapient,
thou art an exile, interlaced
among my genome

(eight blue frocks, selfsame,
sunstiff on a clothesline
under the still windmill)

Nonhomologous
gene scissoring its way in
to wherever it lands—

thou art an exile
inside each of the hundred
trillion cells of me, an exile

who walks amid the alien
feedcorn & the nursling mares
& dreams in thy sporadic

rearrangements of his own
lunge home—
(backwards

diaspora, toward some plainer
monocelled organism & my
chromosomes' controlled

breakage & insertion into that old—)

      —oh sloth & wrath,
opposite & mortal, transpose
thy base pairs & let me slough thee, jumping

genes, off . . .

—but Babylon, Exile, is risen
in all this meantime, anomie,
vanity, 47-times-split-in-two
cell-swarm, oh that Babylon
is arisen, & shall collapse no

more . . .

FIVE

(Pilgrim's Deviations 5)

Bibliolater, I
like to thumb through the Syllabus of Errors
and the Antonymic Dictionary, their
catalogues of wrongs and unresemblances.

Like clicking over and over
the Seldom Asked Questions'
defunct link:
catechismus
interruptus . . .

And the Shrine's voicemail message
repeats, loop after loop:
We can no longer guarantee
we will answer
due to the overwhelming
volume of your calls . . .

Self-Portrait in Ink

As the gone-
translucent

octopus
jet-blasts into evasion, vanishing

while its ink-sac spurts
a cloud of defensive

mucus & coagulant
azure-black pigment,

self-shaped
octopus imago in ink, so the shark

gnashes at that blobbed
sepia phantom,

pseudomorph
that disperses into black

nebulae & shreds
with each shark-strike

& the escaped
octopus throbs

beyond, see-through
in the see-through water, untouched—:

so, go
little poem, little

ink-smudge-on-fingertip
& -print, mimicker

& camouflage,
self-getaway, cloud-

scribble, write
out my dissipating

name on the water,
emptied sac of self-illusive ink . . .

"Behold, I Am Against the Prophets," Saith the Lord, "Who with Sweet Tongues Say, 'The Lord Saith'"

As once a six-winged seraph lifted, on the altar's tongs,
a lit coal to sear

a prophet's unpurged mouth,
& Ezekiel chewed a papyrus scroll

written outside & in with oversweetened
words of lamentation & song & woe, & slow-

of-tongue Moses,
holy-inhabited, still

stood before Pharaoh quavering
through his *uncircumcised lips*—

so, betongued & vatic, speak of this

spotted rose snapper: through its gills
crawls a parasitic crustacean

tongue-bug, *c. exigua,* hard-
segmented, white-shelled, to fix

its seven pairs of hooks
into the mouth's artery & blood-

suck the fish's tongue down to a stub
to supplant that shrivel

from now on with its own
fastened-on & tongue-rhymed body—

—Let the Spirit of the Lord

speak through thee, and His word
be in thy tongue, be

what tongue thou have,
exoskeletal, lingual & occupying

(Son of Man, eat
what thou findest,

eat this scroll). Peering
out toward incoming

scraps of sustenance
through the snapper's pink, possessed gape, those black

teeth-encaged eyes, that mouth enmouthed . . .

The Parable of the Mustard Seed

*Whereunto shall we liken the kingdom of God? . . . It is like a grain of
mustard seed: which when it is sown in the earth, is less than all the seeds
that be in the earth. But . . . it groweth up, and becometh greater than all
herbs, and shooteth out great branches, so that the fowls of the air may lodge
under the shadow of it.*

—Mark 4:30–32

+Not-yet-irruptive, unparousial noon:
something's nested and indeterminable in the roadside mustard shrub

but there's no *fowle of heaven* lodged and sheltered there.
A thousand black-pellet seeds

reissue and disperse from its gnawed, cruciferous blooms.

+*The tyme is fulfillid, and the kyngdoom*

of God schal come nyy?
But the eschatos, the last one, tarries and sojourns
among alabaster jars of spikenard ointment,
among leperskins and myrrh-bearing women.

+Something's brooded in the lobed-
leafed, hair-spiked
rosettes of birdsrape mustard, something
all consonant, unvowelled and augural, among seeds
germinal and ready to be crushed.

+Now the psalters crumble and lutes fall away.
The scatomancer, for further droppings, watches and abides.

You who exist, be like
those who do not exist, says the Secret Gospel.

+Whereunto shall we liken

this three-foot golden weedtuft mustard shrub,
some grizzled
hatchling's scratched-out hunger cry inside

and then inside?

Say we say it is like the pullulating kingdom—
over the summer-abandoned schoolyard—
of the tough bunched green
fists of unripenable fig.

+Let the crickets take their gutload. Let the mustard
scrub unspill its self-profusion, grain by mote-sized grain.
Let its underleaf warble and unmoving wing-shiver
speak not
without a parable.
Some things only dissimilitude can tell.

Now the knives are at my fatlings' throats. And all things are ready.

Dedication

The dried blood of San Gennaro is said to miraculously liquefy three times a year when it is brought close to the relics of his body

Is this box a reliquary or some other
arcane & ill-touched altar, in which
a shard of centuries-preserved blood
has begun to slosh once more against
its walls, beguiled by distant logorrheic
chants, to reliquefy? Is this the housing
of some prayed-to thing that cannot *but*
be slithering always past our congealing
stare? —Lay jewels, then: embed ebony
& bloodstone in its tiny, unbudged door.

Like unto a Merchant Man Seeking Goodly Pearls

The kingdom of heaven is like unto a merchant man, seeking goodly pearls:
Who when he had found one pearl of great price, he went and sold all that
he had, and bought it.

—Matthew 13:45–46

The most beautiful pearl is only the brilliant sarcophagus of a worm.

—Raphael Dubois

I A.

Some mother-of-pearl icon of undesire:
lead Buddha jammed deep into an oyster's
pried-open valves to make it secrete
spherical layers of overlapping nacre
in the shape of that bloated and placid intruder,
like a larval fluke of great price, jewel-interred.

"A derangement of the mollusk's normal state":
the pearl sac's iridescence against the grit
of this boring-in and walled-off irritant,
some holy, unejectable foreign object
(the Torah's word for *holy* means "set apart").
The pearl-formation's "pathological, not intelligent,"

defensive layers of the flesh-flap mantle's
occult and all-concentric blister pearl
half-flattened, half-domed-over, hemispherical,
encysting in a thousand tiers the Buddha, internal-
leaden, quasi-parasitical,
sarcophagus splendid as a worm's. *The pearl*

of GREAT cost—why get that? my son insisted,
Why not just pick out one that's lower-priced
and save a little bit of money for food?

I B.

"I want to find that sweet spot, and go there"
the neurosurgeon said, and planted four
electrodes deep-brain in each hemisphere,
the dura mater exposed through the burr-
holes into the skull to leave a stimulator
in pearl-sized brain Area 25, hyper-

agitant. Though the mechanism's "incompletely understood"
there's still a "sudden disappearance of the void"
twenty seconds after switching on electrodes
with "spaghetti-sized" wires through the mid-
brain, then what these melancholics have never had:
an unmistakable draining of their dread.

And so "this is a surgical strike"
the neurosurgeon says, with battery packs
implanted along the patient's neck
to deliver through gold and platinum wires a shock
at frequencies and pulsewidths that de-black
the mind. The surgeon says, "This is a surgical strike"

—against apathy, anxiety, despair
that wallow overspiked in the whited matter,
electrified, unslothed at the perfect Hertz . . .

II (A and B) Double Villanelle

Strange, and incompletely understood—
this apathy, anxiety, despair
accreting midbrain as though they could

derange the organism's normal state
by some nacreous icon of undesire
in conchiolin and aragonite.

A sudden disappearance of the void
when the surgeon finds that sweet spot, and shocks there,
and says, "This really *is* a kind of mind

control": these unejectable holy objects
of electrodes buried in each hemisphere,
till "suddenly they hit the spot," the patient

said (extravagant pearl, neuronal sphere of God)
"and everything lit up." Bypassing the four
strange and incompletely understood

gospels, parable-garbled, and antisoulants
that overspike all through the white matter
and derange the disordered spirit's promised state.

Oh Kingdom of Heaven, Buddha in the mind,
pry open my valves and make them secrete
that sensation of a disappearing void.

I'd sell everything I own, to seize on this:
that imitation-pearl-walled leaden figure,
that alien, unejectable holy object.

Or that foreign and unknowable inner subject:
a derangement of the psyche's normal state
by a sudden elimination of its void:
strange and incomplete, but understood.

As in a Dim Scriptorium

[1]

—As if always
in some dim scriptorium, with inkhorn's

ear wax & honey & piss

pigment to ornament with gold
the flesh side of outspread vellum.

As if scrambling always to catch

up with a cantor's syntax, inflection
in Latin vowels of gospel & psalm

till my wrist & palm spasm & ribs

cramp my lungs when I lean
to scribble before those inviolable

syllables dissolve into air like my every

breath-fume over the restless quill
as its nib punctures again

the ice-crust of crystal reforming on the inkwell—

[2]

In-
attend, conscripted

& ever-distracted

monk-scribe: *What*
is the Kingdom of God like?

And whatever I've misheard or already
forgotten, reglazing with gold my own marginal gloss,

thumps hail-dull around me:

In parables . . . the man goes in with his sickle . . .
like a treasure buried in a field . . . like a woman with yeast . . .

[3]

What is the Kingdom of God like? Like

(go in with your sickle)
a dim scriptorium

where many-written & half-heard words
are mouthed beyond all attention,
swan quill stilled, dripping with gall & lampblack

ink. As if there were permissible
transcriptions of inattention,

missals riddled with elisions

to mark them aside (as if
in wax & urine & honey's

gold emblazing)

as unscriptable & dumbfounded: twice-blessed.

Extremophilic Magnificat

Awe . . . was an awful Mother, but I liked him better than none.
—Emily Dickinson

(I)
Pompeii Worm
—*Alvinella pompejana*, discovered 1980

This near-boiling geyser-gush through the Earth's crust
blasted water
acidic as vinegar
on Galapagos' seabed, this

papery tube the extremophile
Pompeii worm drills
to make its habitation in a black-
smoker hydrotherm rift-zone chimney

with its tentacles of scarlet head-gills
in cold seeps
fifty degrees
and its tail at the tube-mouth six inches

away in a hundred-
degree-more-torrid
spew
through
the slab waving the feathers of a gray

shawl made wholly
out of symbiotic bacteria
into and out of the magma—

Theo-
phobe,

what can *you*
do
with these creatures, these
living filaments that fur the worm's back and feed
off sugared mucus   it oozes

and repay their host by denitrifying,
sulfur-eating, detoxifying
the sulfide   jets so pressured by   the mile-
deep sea they can't break into boil?

(II)
Bone-eating Snotflower
—Osedax mucofloris, discovered 2002

Lord, Theos, down here they call those   monstrous bodies *hopeful*
     whose
genetic spasms of deformation
amount to a *saltation*,
a leap   into a wholly new species

Evolution's   random hypervariation
I call it *theurgy*   God-work
like thy
eye-

less, mouth-   less, ungutted bone-devourers
in their sheaths
of mucus on whale-fall carcasses
translucent tubes'   red plumage

of hemoglobin   with bone-
embedded
egg-

sac and root-tendrils plundering the whale
skulls' fats and oils.

There on the abyssal plain   the larvae
that unhatch themselves onto a sunk   whale skeleton
grow immediately female and hollow
out the marrow

their three-inch pink   stalk
boring in to colonize   the carcass' eye-
socket bone. But the ones that implant
themselves on a female snot-

flower's   body instead stay as they are
microscopic   male and paedomorphic
left-over   scraps of their yolk-

sac the only nourishment   they ever get . . .
A hundred subvisible males
lie sheathed inside one female
("The most dramatic sexual dimorphism   in the animal
      kingdom")

They stay larval
always
and brimming   with sperm
Flesh of the flesh of her
who is bone to the sperm

whale's sucked-dry bone . . .

(III)
Annunciation to Mary, and Her Hymn of Praise the Magnificat
—Luke 1

Hail, bulged   ovisac and dwarf male
mucofloris,

paper
tube from boil
to chill,

the Lord is with thee   too, in involuntary
sanctifying
at the vent-site, and toxin-purifying
eurytheotic
me, like

a symbiont feathered along my spine   like your green
bone-roots   suckling on marrow-fat . . .
Our bodies—bacterial-
fuzzed and toxin-eating, scald-

loving, tentacles over a hundred
thousand eggs surrounded
by a swarm of third-
of-a-millimeter
males—do   *magnify the Lord* whether or not we want them to . . .

To enter the ribbed and Gothic   chambers of whale skeleton and
     take
root there, or
to wash between extremes, poison and cure . . .
Theophobe, are you me   are we rhyme-sounds, do we

rhyme with these
creatures
I don't want to know. *The universe
is the answer,*
a particle physicist said, *but damned   if we know the question* . . .

Should we
keep
all these things in the depths   as if we'd never
spoken of them, or call   ourselves hopeful

monsters like these, un-
fathom
all they say   as they wave
pink gill-plumes over
their gray and brain-shaped ovaries?

SIX

(Pilgrim's Deviations 6)

For the zeroth time I have told you what I mean.

What's the escape velocity from a mind
whose gravity hauls anything
that approaches into involuntary
and inconclusible orbit?

Find me that vagrant ecstasis,
that stepping-out, unmortified.

Exeunt everyone, though go
carefully,
if at all: the radio
says the Stagnation
Warning remains all year in effect, so what here's

theomorphic, here among the violable
sanctums, the
uncovered ground contaminants:
sackcloths and scourges
prepacked for those who dare to leave the Shrine.

Do you know the skeleton key's
illimitable access

derives wholly from the scraping-
off of all its bits
that otherwise might catch?

You: unphylumable,
self-ridding, unordained, toward Whom
all our blessings relentlessly reflow, de-
deify Thyself
and finger me again and again like a paternoster:

this is the Dismissal.
The Mass is ended. Go Thou in peace.

Six Notes Toward the End

The sestina is a dangerous experiment . . . It is a mantrap . . .
—F. Hueffer, *Macmillan's,* 1881

[1]

Say your last words now, insistent as a cut,
like Revelation's end-obsession in their relentless 6-6-6.

I have hated the way this form assembles: terminal.
-*Cide* means kill. As in *decide.* Six-sided,

inexorable and unstable as a die,
the form rehearses and rehearses its hearse-ridden ending.

[2]

I have hated the coming-together-again of the endings
like the seamed discontinuities of a jump cut.

Every stanza, again intwisted, that dun word *die.*
Keep saying, keep enacting, the same stuck six

confabulations of conclusion, like unfolded insides
of some wadded-up suicide note, its frantic, undebatable terms.

[3]

Who keeps passing through that midnight terminal
in the mind, its clanked-in-place iron gates, the shrill ends

of gone-off train whistles in tunnel-flash, the sighed
airblast of unstoppable cars, the cut-

off schedule of arrivals, the anti-sext,
midnight's-prayer-for-noon, the disobeyed orders of *die*?

[4]

All the last notes, the drilled ultimate words, the dead-
ends of the said: we come, don't we always, to their terms.

Of obscure origin, my dictionary says, of an ancient link between *sex*
   and *six.*
Driven here, as in sex, by some promise of pleasure-shaped ending—

body over practiced body, like hesitation cuts'
rehearsal for some perfectible suicide.

[5]

Half-side-lit, inarticulable, something has sidled
close to you, something having its own death

in mind. You let it nuzzle you in the dark, cut
off for once from all that indeterminate

continuance, here where the ends
must teem, here in the roll of six

[6]

six-sided cross-occurrences of six
aleatory tumblings toward egocide

as if I could rest at last on a single end
or decide all by myself the way the die

should still. As if surrender's terms
could ever be agreed-on, or *being* be
                              edited down through some unexpectable cut.

To Revoke All Wills and Codicils
Heretofore Made by Me

I.

And I have come unwillingly, bearing
so little

you could want:
let me pass,

I have come
obliteratively,

obituary-
bearing

toward the glyptic
beryls in your bone-box

—What:
did you think

that *otherwise*
this would end, Ought-Still-to-Be?

II.

Let's each
heap at least the graven
pillars that divide us with split

honeycombs and lamb's
spleen and blood, and garlands

of lamb's-ear for Terminus, implacable

god of all our severing.

III.

Deep in the spleen, red pulp, white pulp,

this sanguinous-formation, this
hematopoiesis and reservoir
of not-yet-re-pulsed blood, like
the indwelling of the thought

ought-never, ought-never, ought-never-
have-taken-

place . . .

IV.

And now must even more be brought
through gush
on gush to term? We just
got past that other
past, a half
century of it, unplumbable,
unmine, plu-
perfect, beyond
every understanding
of yours oh God
of all our severings.

And by then its meanings had long
already been
deceased, all yester-

-shriven,

-riven.

V.

Where is our
time signature, the
quaver by the clef,
by which we're told
where a beat is heard, a thousand

sperm germinating

in the course of one heartbeat,
the tempus imperfectum, the cut
time, inconclusive
cadences of the credos—

God is
agápē, God is agape:

VI.

God of all our severings including this
continuous
interminus:
now now
not now

now
not
this

twi-
dim this
demi-

night this

shivering in the invisibly webbed air this

naught

VII.

The Heraclitean
Fragments stutter
that the kosmos is an ever-

unkindling and re-
kindling, self-

de-ceasing

fire that ever-
has-been and will-be,
all thought-burnt
gall and choler and bile:

desist, at once, Flame, cease, out-
sputter—

VIII.

Autumn's the spleen season,
says the Treatise,

season of up-bubbling
black mud and in-

bubbling black
bile, the negative

teleology of middle age
offered up.

Hard anymore to remember
the last time time

seemed to last
its own uninterrogated while.

Now the long shrine-walk back
to the present, the literal, its

daily obliteration and up-bubbling
being,

half-enough.
Middle age, says the Treatise, is also the season of spleen.

IX.

He was like, "Fuck off, fuck-
hole," and I was like, "Like shit
I WILL," then he was like

We were all
like, not quite
what we were.
In the midst of
something, inflected
by it, like a schwa. *Selva*
oscura;

obscurable selves.

Since last midnight the password expired, access
will henceforward be denied.

You must change, the popup
wizard said, the intimate
questions that guard your entry.

A new password must contain
more unorthodox punctuation,

punctations, for the gushed
pneumatology of your going-in.

X.

That it might pass, it comes—

full-voweled,
full-
consonantal

rhyme of exit-wound with entry-wound, identically gash-

bordered: it comes
to pass.

So *what was*
must not be
again, and now
what must

not be is. And just
in time the bay wind debrides
these wakes' sparks

of their salt and gleam. Which the air now
gives.
     Gives
over. Only
in time,
only to it.

XI.

What *are* we like, like
rhymes that won't
complete, like streams

dammed, and
the maelstrom of their blockage,
like rheum, like rooms
blown-through, like months
uncatchably offflown?

Or like *list,*
list: it used

to mean *desire,* like *lust,*
like *lascivious*—

Listen for the terminal
music, the   germinal
near mer-
    ger
of the opposite-
       meant,
off-rhyme of *obscure*
      and *clear,*
   meant
and *recondite.*

The recording interspersing
the Muzaked hymn

keeps telling me (wrongly) I may
experience

a few periods

of silence.

List, list

to these
mete-

d out unsamenesses:

—Must
the luster
    hover
only over

the *empty* tomb?

        —The rejected
passages marked in red,

but the holy ones, also, marked
                            in red.

—Will there be

another testament,
    or is this one it?

XII.

This turbulent
passage out of doubt
through the worshippable
oblique, where
so little

otherwise abides—

Did you think that otherwise
it would end?

No-Longer-Being, drip
heavier on me, as

around us on a rain-ripped spiderweb
what never *came* to be
squirms and colliquesces,

like the dragonfly my son fed into it,
disintegrated, wing-wadded,
dangling

by one jerking, thrice-wrapped leg.

XIII.

Never-Been, hoard
for me your jeweled sword.
Yet-to-Come, yet
to come, run

me through.

Notes

As if the exegesis could ever cease

Pilgrim's Deviations 1:
Nones: from Latin for *ninth*, the ecclesiastical prayer-service said at the ninth hour of the day, or 3 P.M.

All Saints:
xenotransplantation: transplanting cells or tissues from one species to another.

Pilgrim's Deviations 2:
heterographs: the same letter used to represent different sounds.

The Kingdom of God Is Not Usher'd In with Pomp and Exclamations:
The title is Luke 17:20 in the Mace New Testament translation of 1729.

Sunrise Insomnia Service:
The story of the apostles' sleep in the garden of Gethsemane the night before the crucifixion is told in Matthew 26.

Stray Apostrophes:
Eyheh asher ehyeh: Hebrew אהיה אשר אהיה—What God answers when Moses asks His name (Exodus 3:14). An untranslatable phrase variously translated as "I am who am," "I am who I am," "I am Being," "I will become whatsoever I please," "I shall prove to be."

Reading the Not-Written:
The italicized quotations are from *The Apocryphon of James.*

Genomic Vanitas—
Vanitas:
Endure their going hence: "Men must endure their going hence, even as their coming hither; ripeness is all," Shakespeare, *King Lear*, 5, 2.

Vocation:
exon & intron, code and junk: An exon is "the region of a gene that contains the code for producing the gene's protein. Each exon codes for a specific portion of the complete protein. In some species (including humans), a gene's exons are separated by long regions of DNA (called introns or sometimes "junk DNA") that have no apparent function." (National Human Genome Research Institute)

Void Domiciles:
phenylanine, glutamine, arginine, Stop: Phenylanine, glutamine, and arginine are among the twenty amino acids. "Each specific sequence of three DNA bases (called a codon) codes for one amino acid. GCA codes for the amino acid alanine, and AGA codes for arginine" (Carine Dennis and Richard Gallagher, *The Human Genome*). "Sixty-one of the sixty-four possible codons correspond to specific amino acids; the other three are 'stop' signals that tell the ribosomes to stop adding amino acids to the protein." (Alvin Silverstein, et al., *DNA)*

that will be shed for you: Matthew 26:28, "For this is my blood of the New Testament, which shall be shed for many unto remission of sins."

psychopomp: one who conducts souls to the other world.

How came you here to linger in the gloomy shade and *My own unspeakable excess in wine* are from Book 11 of the *Odyssey,* where Odysseus confronts in the land of the dead the shade of his dead companion Elpenor.

Mother Tongue:
dittography: accidental or erroneous duplication of words or letters in writing or printing.

Nihil obstat: Latin, "nothing to hinder": the phrase used by the official Roman Catholic censor to indicate that a publication has been examined and contains nothing damaging to faith or morals.

Nature sometimes draws aside & goes / away: Gerald of Wales (1147–1223).

Memento Vivi:
genome of the Plague: J. Parkhill, et al., "Genome sequence of *Yersina pestis,* the causative agent of plague," *Nature* 413, October 4, 2001.

And in this flea our two bloods mingled be: John Donne, "The Flea."

The plague full swift goes by; / I am sick, I must die: Thomas Nash, "Litany in Time of Plague."

Do this in memory: I Corinthians 11:24: "Take, eat: this is my body, which is broken for you: this do in remembrance of me."

base pairs: "The bases are the 'letters' that spell out the genetic code. In DNA, the code letters are A, T, G, and C, which stand for the chemicals adenine, thymine, guanine, and cytosine, respectively. In base pairing, adenine always pairs with thymine, and guanine always pairs with cytosine." (National Human Genome Research Institute)

telomeres: repetitive DNA sequences at the ends of chromosomes that help to protect the chromosome.

Canticle of the Creatures:
& the unclean spirits went out . . . . : Mark 5:13, where Jesus expels from a possessed man a demonic spirit that then enters into a herd of swine and causes them to throw themselves off a cliff.

Reading About Retrotransposons in Amish Country, in the Fall:
Retrotransposons: a form of transposon, which was discovered in the pioneering studies by Barbara McClintock with corn plants. Transposons, or "jumping genes," are sequences of genetic material that can transplant themselves from one place to another within a chromosome. Jennifer Atkinson writes, in *Chance in the House of Fate: A Natural History of Heredity,* that "the DNA of virtually every known species is inhabited by wandering genes able to cut themselves out of one chromosome and splice themselves into another . . . Some of these vagrant bits of DNA may be remnants of viral genes that once wormed their way into the genomes of bacteria, plants, animals. As it turns out, jumping genes

dart not only from spot to spot within a genome, but from organism to organism, species to species, plant to insect to mammal."

For yea, ye shall be strangers, and also exiles: 2 Samuel 15:19.

point mutation: a kind of mutation in which a single base nucleotide is replaced by another nucleotide in a genetic sequence.

"Behold, I Am Against the Prophets," Saith the Lord, "Who with Sweet Tongues Say, 'The Lord Saith'":
The title is a version of Jeremiah 23:31.

The stories of the calling-to-prophecy of Isaiah, Ezekiel, and Moses are told in Isaiah 6, Ezekiel 2–3, and Exodus 3–4, respectively.

"Let the spirit of the Lord speak through thee, and His word be in thy tongue": 2 Samuel 23:2.

Son of Man, eat what thou findest, eat this scroll: Ezekiel 3:1.

The Parable of the Mustard Seed:
"The tyme is fulfillid, and the kyngdoom of God schal come nyy" is from Mark 1:15, in the *Wycliffe Bible* (1395) translation.

Scatomancer: one who performs divination by examination of animal feces.

Secret Gospel: The Apocryphon (or "Secret Book") of James, from the Nag Hammadi Library.

"Now the knives are at my fatlings' throats. And all things are ready": cf. Matthew 22:4.

Like unto a Merchant Man Seeking Goodly Pearls:
Helen S. Mayberg, et al., "Deep Brain Stimulation for Treatment-Resistant Depression," *Neuron* 45, 651–660, 2005.

A derangement of the mollusk's normal state: "It appears that the pearl is not a product of health associated with undisturbed conditions, but results from a derangement in the normal state of the mollusk. Unable to resist, to rid itself of the opposing evil, it exercises the powers given to it by a beneficent Creator and converts the pain into perfection, the grief into glory." (George Frederick Kunz and Charles Hugh Stevenson, *Book of the Pearl: The History, Art, Science, and Industry of the Queen of Gems*)

pathological, not intelligent: "This walling-out of intruders is not the result of intelligent forethought or of instinct . . . it is a pathological rather than intelligent action." (Kunz and Stevenson, *Book of the Pearl*)

subgenual cingulate: brain region where Area 25 is found.

As in a Dim Scriptorium:
scriptorium: a room in a monastery where manuscripts were read aloud and copied by scribes.

What is the Kingdom of God like?: Mark 4:30.

Extremophilic Magnificat:
"*The universe is the answer, but damned if we know the question*": Leon Lederman, *The God Particle*.

flesh of the flesh of her / who is bone to the sperm // whale's sucked-dry bone: Adam's hymn of praise for Eve in Genesis 2:23: "This is now bone of my bones, and flesh of my flesh."

Six Notes Toward the End:
sext: from Latin for "six," canonical service at the sixth hour of the day, or noon.

Acknowledgments

Enormous thanks to the editors of the following journals where these poems originally appeared:

Colorado Review: "As in a Dim Scriptorium";
FIELD: "All Saints," "'Behold, I Am Against the Prophets,' Saith the Lord, 'Who with Sweet Tongues Say, "The Lord Sayeth"'," "Extremophilic Magnificat," "The Parable of the Mustard Seed";
Denver Quarterly: "The Scale by Which the Mapped Concerns the Map";
Electronic Poetry Review: "Dedication," "Theme and Invariants";
Free Verse: "Like unto a Merchant Man Seeking Goodly Pearls";
Gettysburg Review: "Having Read the Holy Spirit's Wikipedia";
Hotel Amerika: "To Revoke All Wills and Codicils Heretofore Made by Me";
Image: Art, Faith, Mystery: "Sunrise Insomnia Service";
The Kenyon Review: "Genomic Vanitas," "Reading the Not-Written," "Pilgrim's Deviations";
New American Writing: "Stray Apostrophes," "Six Notes Toward the End";
Poetry Northwest: "Year's End Paradoxography";
Southern Review: The Kingdom of God Is Not Usher'd In with Pomp and Exclamations";
TriQuarterly: "Valedictions";
Virginia Quarterly Review: "Self-Portrait in Ink."

"Self-Portrait in Ink" was reprinted in *The Pushcart Prize XXXI: Best of the Small Presses* (2007); on *Poetry Daily* (www.poems.com), and in *The Long Journey: Contemporary Northwest Poets,* edited by David Biespiel (Oregon State University Press, 2006).

"Canticle of the Creatures" from "Genomic Vanitas" was reprinted on *Verse Daily* (www.versedaily.org).

Enormous thanks, too, to Peter Conners for his editorial care and enthusiasm and support of this book, and to friends who have read these poems in many earlier drafts and offered readings and advice: Tim Liu, Dan Tobin, Bill Wenthe, Brenda Miller, Don Platt. And to Thor Hansen, who first taught me about *Toxoplasma gondii*, Alba the glowing rabbit, the tongue bug, and many other creatures of monstrous extremity.

About the Author

Bruce Beasley grew up in Macon, Georgia, and studied at Oberlin College (B.A., 1980), Columbia University (M.F.A., 1982), and the University of Virginia (Ph.D., 1993). He is the author of six previous collections of poems, including *The Corpse Flower: New and Selected Poems* (University of Washington Press, 2007), *Lord Brain* (winner of the University of Georgia Press Contemporary Poetry Series Award, 2005), and *Summer Mystagogia*, selected by Charles Wright for the 1996 Colorado Prize for Poetry. He has won fellowships from the National Endowment for the Arts and the Artist Trust and three Pushcart prizes, and his work appears in *The Pushcart Book of Poetry: The Best Poems from the First Thirty Years of the Pushcart Prize*. He lives in Bellingham, Washington, with his wife the poet and nonfiction writer Suzanne Paola and their son Jin, and is a professor of English at Western Washington University.

BOA Editions, Ltd.
American Poets Continuum Series

Colophon

Theophobia, poems by Bruce Beasley,
is set in Adobe Garamond, a digital font designed in 1989
by Robert Slimbach (1956–) based on the French Renaissance roman
types of Claude Garamond (ca. 1480–1561) and the italics of
Robert Granjon (1513–1589).

The publication of this book is made possible, in part,
by the special support of the following individuals:

Anonymous
Anne Germanacos
X. J. & Dorothy M. Kennedy
Katherine Lederer
Tony Leuzzi
Dan Meyers, in honor of Steve Russell
Boo Poulin
Deborah Ronnen & Sherman Levey
Steven O. Russell & Phyllis Rifkin-Russell
Ellen & David Wallack
Glenn & Helen William